# CONQUER THE TELEPHONE MONSTER®

Orion Abbot-Davies

# CONQUER THE TELEPHONE MONSTER

Grab a phone and grow
your business **now!**

# Contents

# Acknowledgement:

I must acknowledge a number of people in connection with the writing of this book: Rodger Scott, Alison Maugham, Adrian Edmonds, Ann Hobbs and Ben Mears for their support, encouragement and inspiration. My wife Lizzie for her unconditional love and assistance and the endless sacrifices she made so that this book could become a reality. My sister Latifah for her amazing kindness and generosity. Last but not least I want to thank my daughter Lily, my little star and my inspiration.

# My telemarketing journey

As a young boy growing up, I remember watching my father in wonder as he used the phone to manage his businesses and talk to his friends and acquaintances. I marvelled at his apparently effortless skill and confidence and could not imagine how anyone could pick up a phone and be so charming, convincing and effective. He always seemed to get exactly what he wanted and people were happy to give it to him.

As I went on to start businesses of my own, I developed my own phone skills but was still amazed by people that seemed to make it look so easy. When the global recession of 2008 hit the UK I was managing a growing online retail business. We had just opened our first small shop in a mall in Bristol and within three months we lost everything. Along with thousands of other businesses we had been wiped out and I had to part ways with my business partners and find work fast. I took the first job available which was in a small, local telemarketing business. The work was hard and the environment was brutal with staff hired and fired on a weekly basis but I kept my head down and persevered.

After putting my time in at this telemarketing company, I then had an opportunity to work at a much more prestigious full service B2B (business to business) marketing agency, which I jumped on. The only catch with this job was that it was a one hundred and forty mile daily commute which would eat up a large chunk of my salary but, as it was such an amazing opportunity, I seized it. They wasted no time putting me to work and, almost immediately, I was calling for a large technology account with a complex multi-million-pound offering. My mission was to generate high level appointments for the client's sales force with the top people in some of the largest global businesses in the world. It was a wonderful responsibility to be trusted with so quickly but it was also made very clear that my job security was directly tied to the success of this account. This was a very clever move on their part as no one else in the company was allowed to call on this account but me. This made me feel like a genuine stakeholder in the business. I owned a little piece of it and because of that I worked as hard as I could to make it a success.

It was here that I began to be encouraged, for the first time, to use qualities like charm, empathy, intuition and my own innate intelligence to generate leads instead of the brainless, bullying tactics typical of so many "phone basher" telemarketing businesses. It was also here that I accidentally discovered a very compelling reason to want to work for myself. I was looking for stationary one day in the company's store cupboard. I remember I pulled out a notepad and a printed sheet of paper with the word "CONFIDENTIAL" fell into my hand. It was a price list of the company's services that included what they were charging their clients for everyone in my department's services. There it was in black and white. They were literally charging ten times what they were paying me, per day, for the telemarketing services I was delivering and I wasn't even on commission!

I think it was in that moment that I decided to start my own telemarketing business as soon as possible. I was, however, still learning so much in this job so I decided to keep my head down for the time being and learn as much as I could. I'm proud to say I achieved some really big wins during my time there but eventually the long commute took its toll and I decided to look for work closer to home. I was fortunate enough to quickly find a job as a home-based telemarketing manager for a relatively small but rapidly growing telecoms wholesaler. This was a very exciting and in some ways very anarchic business to be a part of.

The day I met the charismatic young MD of that company, he said:

"Listen mate, we don't know anything about tele-marketing. You're the expert so do what you like. So long as you get results, I don't care how you go about it."

What an opportunity! My previous employer had been far nicer to work for than some others but they had a very structured way of doing things which, at times, I found somewhat restrictive. I love optimising, innovating and automating wherever possible. If I could see a way to do something in a day that used to take a week I would just get on and do it. Here was a rare chance to develop every idea I'd had to streamline the process of phone based lead generation. I got to work putting together my own set of best practices and soon started seeing some great results. In a year and a half I generated leads for the business worth millions of pounds which helped them grow rapidly.

Eventually one of their main competitors bought them out. This much larger business then acquired a separate telemarketing business and I was given the choice to move to another part of the country and become part of that company, or take redundancy. I took the generous redundancy offer and decided this was the moment to start my own telemarketing business. They also let me keep all the phone equipment I had been using which was an enormous help.

I created Abbot-Davies Associates, initially as a sole trading telemarketing business and then as a limited company, and found my first few clients through word of mouth and referrals from past work colleagues, friends and family. The work was varied and rewarding but I was aware that I would need a more sustainable way to find regular work and build a good reputation. This was when I discovered business networking and its amazing potential for helping start-up enterprises like mine.

The first group I went to was called Working Breakfast. This was a Bristol-based organisation with meetings every few weeks in local hotels and business centres. Here members would introduce their businesses to each other over breakfast and trade referrals to potential clients as well as share useful information about their industries. This particular group was very focused on building genuine friendships between its members which meant you could really trust the referrals you were given and clients could trust you when you were referred to them. I tried other groups but struggled to find anywhere else as friendly or full of genuinely helpful and encouraging people.

One of the things they suggested was that I offer telemarketing training and I followed their advice and instantly fell in love with it. Providing telemarketing services to clients can be a very rewarding activity but positive feedback isn't usually instant. With training, however, you can immediately see if you have made a difference. It was also around this time that I started writing this book as a way to pass on the knowledge I had accumulated over the years and as a support to the workshops. My reputation as a trainer grew and eventually South Gloucestershire Council commissioned me to do regular workshops at the Bristol & Bath Science Park which was a really good way for me to spread the word and help people from all walks of life Conquer the Telephone Monster®. It was also around this time that my Working Breakfast mentors suggested I trademark my slogan hence the mark you can see here.

This brings us to today and the book you are reading! If I had a time machine I would travel back to 2008 and hand this book to myself. This really is everything you need to know to just get on and generate real leads on the phone and I hope it helps you conquer YOUR telephone monster!

## A note about Excel:

This book assumes you are familiar with Microsoft Excel but are not necessarily a "super user". All the formulas, conditional formatting and settings mentioned here are included and ready to use in the spreadsheet that forms part of the resource pack. You can download the resource pack by scanning the QR code below:

Or by going to: abbot-davies.com/resource-pack

Password: **workshop**

## A note about GDPR, ePrivacy and CTPS:

There are certain rules that govern who you can call, how you obtain your prospects permission to contact them and what your responsibilities are regarding their data. These must be taken into account in any multi-channel marketing campaign you do. Some people see them as a barrier, especially with the addition of GDPR in May 2018 but I see them as a vital step towards making B2B telemarketing a more welcome and respectable activity. The days of phone bashing through thousands of random prospects – without thinking about the real value that your offering may bring a business or the rights that your prospects have regarding the data you have on them – are over. This is something I have been preaching from my little soap box for years and it does seem that things are finally changing for the better.

**The Corporate Telephone Preference Service (CTPS)** is an opt out register that lets businesses choose not to receive unsolicited sales and marketing telephone calls. Before you call a business you need to make sure they aren't CTPS registered. When you buy data from reputable data vendors such as Experian and Credit Safe you can usually request that it be CTPS checked so this isn't something that should be too much of an obstacle.

**GDPR and ePrivacy** are a set of rules that govern the methods that you can use to contact your prospects and the specifics of your responsibilities regarding their data. Prior to May 2018 it was sufficient to offer an unsubscribe link on the emails you sent to businesses and businesses could choose to stay on your marketing list or not. Now, (and this is something quite a lot of businesses still get wrong...) not only do you have to get each individual that you contact in a business to **explicitly opt in** to receiving your email but you also can't hold on to their contact details for more than eighteen months, **or less than that** if the initial reason you contacted them was for a time limited event or promotion. If you run a six month campaign then, once it is over, you have to delete the contact details of everyone who opted in to receiving your email for that campaign. You also have to be able to send anyone who requests it **every detail** you hold about them **including** any notes you have made about any conversations you had with them. This must be done within a reasonable timeframe and, if they request it, you must delete all of the data you have about this person.

**Most importantly:** From a telemarketing perspective, GDPR **does not** require you to obtain an opt in for either a **B2B cold call** or a regular **B2B communication sent through the post**. Its key focus is on B2B emails and SMS messages. You do, however, need to be able to demonstrate that your call is of "legitimate interest" to the recipient and you cannot make a large amount of unsolicited B2B calls to the same business where they have not opted in to receiving your communications. What constitutes a large amount of B2B calls is difficult to say but, if you've been calling every other day for two weeks and no one has returned your calls, you've probably crossed the line already. Thankfully, If you are calling to offer a business a product or service that you believe could be valuable and of genuine benefit to them then that is considered a "legitimate interest".

Further information can be found at:

en.wikipedia.org/wiki/General_Data_Protection_Regulation

en.wikipedia.org/wiki/EPrivacy_Regulation_(European_Union)

www.tpsonline.org.uk/tps/whatiscorporatetps.html

*"Whatever you can do, or dream you can, begin it. Boldness has genius, power and magic in it."*

Goethe

# Introduction

There it is... The telephone.

Whether it's a desktop phone or a smartphone or even a "soft" phone on your desktop or laptop; you know you have to pick it up and use it but it's just so daunting, isn't it? Questions float in the air...

- **Who** do I call?
- **What** do I say?
- **How** do I keep track?
- **How** do I stay positive?

These "Monsters" are in your way... How do you conquer them? The answer is one you will, no doubt, have heard before: **one at a time**.

This book will guide you through the process of dealing with these monsters **step by step**. It provides a detailed look at everything you will need to create and manage a successful telemarketing campaign of any size from scratch.

Once you know...

- What companies to approach
- Who the best person to talk to is
- What to say to gatekeepers and prospects
- How to respond to what they say
- How to easily manage all those interactions

...then the rest is just practice.

# The
# "Who do I call?"
## Monster

There are many different factors that could define an ideal prospect for your business.

The **key** is to really try to understand who those prospects are and then focus as clearly as possible on those types of potential clients. It may be tempting to say that **anyone** could be an ideal client for you or your business but it makes sense, especially if your resources are limited, to start with the prospects who are most likely to want your services. The more you refine your focus, the greater the potential value of each call.

# Make sure the shoe fits

So how do you find the right kind of business to call? The first step to conquering this monster is to put yourself in the shoes of the various types of enterprises you want to approach. This is particularly true if you are a small, relatively unknown business, with a service or product that you want to introduce to other businesses. In my experience global companies often tend to look for global service providers and local businesses will often prefer to buy from other local businesses. Having a good understanding of the size of the businesses that will most likely want your offering is vital to the success of your campaign. This doesn't mean that a small business will never attract a large one. In fact, sometimes working with a small, nimble business which doesn't cost as much as a bigger, more established player can be a great advantage to a larger company, but the shoe has to fit.

Trying to put yourself in the mindset of your prospects is actually not that hard to do. Think of your own situation. Is there a telemarketing call aimed at your business that you would welcome right now? Many people might answer "No! I hate them! I never want ANY telemarketing calls" and given what a pest telemarketing calls can be, you can hardly blame them. The thing is actually, there is a telemarketing call we would all love to receive at any time, day or night. Even at three in the morning as I experienced myself many years ago!

Before the disastrous world-wide economic crash of 2008, I used to run a successful online retail business called **Cool Glowy Things**. We sold unusual items sourced from all over the world and so long as it was "cool", "glowy" and a "thing" we were happy to sell it. I would spend hours researching anything and everything that might fit that criteria. It could be a simple glow stick for just a few pennies or a handcrafted Italian blown glass lamp for hundreds of pounds. I was particularly interested in items from Japan as that amazing culture always had such a vibrant and fascinating array of unusual goods on offer. The problem was communication and timing. The only phrase I really know in Japanese is **"Hachi-gatsu ga ichiban atsui n desu"** (August is the hottest month) which is only really useful once a year... Also time zone differences made calling at appropriate times quite tricky. This essentially made it hard to have business discussions with most Japanese suppliers. I left my details with a lot of businesses there and had some success but it was always an uphill struggle.

One night I was woken up at three am by my phone ringing. Still half asleep, I answered and a nervous sounding man asked to speak to me by name. I confirmed it was me and was about to give him an earful for waking me up when he pre-empted me and sounding quite flustered, profusely apologised for the timing of his call. "I am so sorry to call you now Mr Abbot-Davies. It's midday here but I've just realised it must be three am where you are! I'm sorry I was just looking at your website here in our offices in Tokyo. We manufacture glowing spinning tops and wondered if you would be interested in looking at our catalogue? I'm so sorry, I can call you back later if you like?" I shook off my sleepy head as fast as I could and quickly said "No, that's fine. Don't worry! I've been looking for this sort of product for a while. Would you be able to send me a sample?" We continued our conversation and those glowing spinning tops became a top seller on my site and later in my shop.

I still have one today!

So what does this say about making the shoe fit? Well, here we have a very enterprising telesales person who took the time to research the sort of businesses abroad that might need their products and then contacted those businesses directly. He may even have anticipated that businesses like mine may find it hard to contact Japanese manufacturers. He got the time zones wrong but because he absolutely nailed the kind of product I was interested in, I was instantly willing to listen to his pitch even at three am!

In my experience, it is absolutely true to say that minutes

spent researching your prospects pains and needs will save you hours wasted making calls to the wrong kind of business.

# Understand your prospect's role

Having a good grasp of what a prospect's role actually involves and whether that role will be appropriate to your offering is vital to the success of a call. For example, a "Marketing Product Director" is a completely different role to a "Marketing Communications Director" but some would just see "Marketing" and "Director" and call them both. Let's think of the impact that would have on your time for a second. It takes time to get through to someone at that level; sometimes days or weeks if they are often out of the office or travelling. You finally get through and the contact tells you they have nothing to do with the sort of services you offer.

If you take a little time to understand what each role you are targeting actually does then you will save yourself a lot of time further down the line. Ask yourself if their role is aligned with your offering. An HR Director, for instance, isn't likely to want to talk about supply chain management software or getting a new phone system.

- Do they cover a geographical area relevant to your product or service? What is the range of your offering and also of your sales force? If you are based in

Europe could you realistically go and pitch your product in front of the management team of a Tokyo or New York based company? Also if they decided to buy your product or service could you deliver it and also provide support for it across such a distance?

- Is your prospect at a level within the organisation that is appropriate for the type of engagement you need? Unfortunately many people oversimplify this question. We've all heard the saying "Speak to the organ grinder, not the monkey" but organisations are much more complex than that. The CEO isn't usually the only person that can make purchasing decisions in a business. The key word is "appropriate".

- Does the prospect have direct responsibility for purchasing your type of product or service? If the answer is yes then you're on the right track. Don't let yourself be tempted into believing that you're talking to the right person just because they are responding positively on the phone. Keep going until you are sure you are talking to someone who has the power to make a purchasing decision for the business.

# If you're not sure...

Sometimes you won't find the exact person you need to talk to before you start calling. This is especially true of larger companies. If you don't know who your perfect prospect is then you could start making contact at a junior level and find your way up. You could also start at the top and try to get mandated down. In my experience both strategies can work very well. It really depends on the type of company you are calling.

Starting by contacting the office manager is easier in one respect as they are often more available than more senior staff. You will start the conversation sooner than if you tried to contact people higher up but it may take some time to get to the person you need and you will probably have to pitch your offering to each new person on the way up. This can work well, for instance, with schools where ordinary sounding roles like "Facilities Manager" can actually translate to "Person who selects all the key technology suppliers for the Bursar or Head who isn't very technical". This isn't always true, mind you. Sometimes it can also mean "Person who basically just knows where the keys to the lawnmower shed are". Your mileage, as they say, may vary.

Alternatively, contacting the boss right at the top on your first call may seem intimidating but once you get through you've won half the battle. If they are impressed by your offering they will most likely mandate you down into their business and request/decree that their key staff talk to you. This is a powerful introduction that will often ease your journey to that golden qualified lead. It can work very well with organisations like law firms, for example, where talking directly to a Managing Partner is very effective because they often have excellent connections with all their key staff who otherwise would be very hard to reach. You may take some time to get through to the person at the top but once you're in… you're in!

# Time for a story...
# Pearl diving

**One sunny day**, a young pearl diver called Tane (Tah-Neh) was sitting by the docks admiring his catch. Gazing into his little leather bag he thought, "These are some of the most beautiful pearls I have ever seen". He had to admit it had taken him some time to find the reef where all the conditions would be right for the best pearls to grow. He had studied the currents and learnt the tides so that he could find his way to the best spot but this meant that when he dived down he would have the best chance to find pearls of real value.

As he admired his catch a huge dragnet fishing boat arrived belching smoke and making the jetties rock. A large man with small eyes came off the boat holding a big crate. He saw Tane and laughed "My name is Hiro and my boat has the biggest net of all! Is that all you have little man? Look at what I caught just today!" With that he set down his crate and opened it. Inside Tane could see a big mess of things. There were bits of coral and sand, fish of all kinds, piles of algae and rubbish and lots of tiny underdeveloped clams. The fat man slammed his crate shut and said, "You'll never get anywhere with your little bag!" With that he picked up his crate and waddled off.

Tane noticed that the fat man had not even asked to look inside his "little bag" of pearls. He wondered where this Hiro had gone to find his catch and decided to follow the boat the next day to find out. In the morning he climbed into his little canoe and tied it to the side of Hiro's boat near the back. The huge boat was filthy and its sides were covered in great clumps of algae and other trash. Tane had no trouble using this to disguise himself and his canoe. If anyone looked down they would just see another pile of junk. Soon they were out to sea and Tane saw Hiro lower his giant net and drag it along the sea bed.

He watched all day as the net was brought up again and again. Eventually he cut his canoe loose and let himself float away until Hiro's boat was over the horizon. He dived down to inspect the ocean floor but couldn't see very well because the nets had stirred up so much mud. He went back up and waited a while. When he descended again he was shocked by the scene of devastation below him. There was nothing left where the net had been except debris and dead and dying fish.

He paddled back to shore and spent the next few months watching Hiro coming and going with his big boat. One day Hiro arrived looking very angry. He saw Tane and said "Someone is trying to kill my business! Every day I go out with my big net I catch less and less. I think someone is taking everything before I get there! If this continues I am going to lose my business…" With that Hiro kicked an empty crate and stormed off. Tane decided to investigate! He knew where Hiro had been dragging his net so he paddled out to the spot he had seen before and had a look around. At first glance it did indeed look as if the ocean floor was bare but as he studied it he noticed something move and then disappear. He swam down to the sea bed and peered around to try to see what it could have been. Just then a spirit disciple of Hina, Goddess of the Sea decided to unexpectedly give Tane (and certain other creatures) the ability to temporarily breathe, hear and talk under water…

Tane was very surprised when a voice said "Hey you! What do you think you are doing? Hide, you fool!" He looked down by his feet and saw a little hermit crab waving at him. "The big net will be here again soon. You have to hide! Hey, quick everyone. We need to help this one!" When the little crab said that, suddenly all sorts of stones and shells that had been hidden under the sand started to move and lots of tiny fish, crabs and oysters appeared. One of them said "We have had to learn to hide from the big net. It comes every day so we can never swim around or look for food or meet others like us, so we don't grow very big anymore. You need to find a big shell and dig a hole in the sand quickly so you can hide too." Tane smiled and thanked them for their advice. He then told them about the reef he had found with all the beautiful pearls and drew directions in the sand so they could find it. He was honest with them about being a pearl diver but said that he would only take pearls to people who would look after them and make them even more valuable. The creatures of the sea thanked Tane and swam off to find his reef.

Tane returned to shore and once again looked at his "little bag" of pearls. He thought about Hiro and felt sorry for him that he couldn't see past his initial successes and realise the damage he had caused. Now all the sea creatures Hiro had tried to catch had learned to hide from him or moved away. Tane wondered if Hiro would learn anything himself from this but thought that was unlikely and that Hiro would just become more aggressive and use bigger and bigger nets, work longer and longer hours and hire more and more people till there was nothing left of the ocean floor but rock and sand.

He started to feel sad that there was no way to stop people like Hiro but then thought back to the creatures that spoke to him and realised that, in time, the problem would correct itself. The big boats would eventually see that their nets were coming up empty, as all the creatures learnt better ways to hide from them. At that point they would either have to learn to use more sustainable ways to find what they were looking for or go out of business. WIth that thought Tane smiled, got into his canoe and paddled off to his favourite reef to find some more beautiful pearls.

I hope you enjoyed Tane's story. I wrote it because after

having spent over a decade generating qualified leads on the phone I've learnt that success that goes unexamined can lead to huge problems further down the line. For example, imagine that a business hired someone like Hiro to generate leads for them and gave him a thousand people to call over ten days. After ten days "Hiro" returns with ten appointments booked. Champagne bottles are opened and bonuses awarded. Everyone is happy.

However, because of their aggressive and relentless approach (PPI cold calls anyone?) the business that hired him now have nine hundred and ninety people who hate their brand and would never do business with them. Suddenly the next campaign doesn't work so well and subsequent campaigns fail almost completely. At this point "Hiro" will probably tell his clients that either their messaging or data is wrong or that there are no more leads in that sector. If they had spent a fraction of their time researching the market and really thinking about who actually needs their product, things might have turned out differently. If they had tried to find out where their prospects tended to meet and share information, when to call them and then called a hundred people intelligently instead of a thousand people blindly, they would have much better pearls and a fertile reef to go back to for more…

# Build or buy?

As mentioned in the pearl diver story, when you're trying to find new clients it's tempting to cast your net as widely as possible and haul in thousands of companies all over the country. Many people go for quantity and hope that quality will somehow materialise if they make thousands of calls all over the place. This is like trying to "boil the ocean to catch fish". It mostly ends up being a terribly inefficient strategy that wastes time and only adds to the confusion (it is also a lot more difficult to do this and stay GDPR compliant). Far better to spend a little time intelligently researching businesses that might genuinely want your services and make the effort to really understand their needs.

Once you've decided who and where your best prospects are likely to be, what's next? If you don't have any data you could build it yourself or you could buy it. There are many independent data vendors out there but if you buy it, for instance, from places that specialise in credit checking, the data may be more reliable. As an example at the time of writing this guide the credit checking company **Experian** have an interactive online tool called: **www.b2bprospector.co.uk** which lets you choose exactly what kind of data you need. You can select a large amount of options (geographical location, company size, role etc.) and the amount of contacts they have available and at what price updates automatically. You can then preview the data and, if it matches your expectations, purchase it online. Finally you would then download your data as an Excel spreadsheet.

This can be a very good solution to get you going quickly. One thing to bear in mind however is that, as with any purchased data, many other businesses are also buying it so when you call these numbers it is very likely they will have received a large amount of similar telemarketing calls from these other companies before you. These other companies may also not have been very nice to deal with so there might be a greater level of pushback. In other words, this can make it harder to get through if you are the hundredth telemarketing call that week that they have had to deal with. This is a good argument for building your own data...

# You don't need much to get started

If you do decide to build prospect data yourself it may take a little more time but it's often a lower cost option, all your data will definitely be up to date and you can research and target the businesses you want more personally. So what do you need?

Once you have found a company that is likely to be interested in your offering, what then? What essential pieces of information should you gather before you can pick up the phone and start generating high value leads for your business? Here again the temptation may be to grab as much information about each company as possible (size, turnover, employee count, number of branches, current supplier, address of each office, list of all management level staff etc.). While the aim is ultimately to build the most complete and accurate picture of your prospects as possible you only actually need four pieces of information to get you started:

1. **Company name**
2. **Contact name**
3. **Role**
4. **Direct line**

The first three of these (Company name, Contact name and Role) are essential so that you know who you're trying to contact and can ask for people by name when you call. To find this information you can search for them online either through one of the popular search engines or directly on sites that specialise in listing the details of small and large businesses and their staff. There are literally thousands of these so try to pick a directory that is as local as possible to the area you are trying to target. If you were targeting the Bristol area in the UK for example you could search for "Bristol business directory" and a host of excellent resources would soon be at your fingertips.

The telephone number needs to be the most direct route to your prospect. This could be a mobile or a direct line (also referred to as a Direct Dial In or DDI) or a landline extension. These can be quite hard to get as most switchboards will not give them out and websites tend to only supply one main number. In small companies a main number may be all you need as the boss might answer it but this isn't the case in larger businesses.

Whenever you have a chance you should **always ask for a direct line**. Imagine you are having a conversation with a prospect who is keen and shows some interest in your services but doesn't want to take things further until, for example, after their office move is complete. You could agree a good time for you to call back and at the same time ask if there's a direct line you could take down for them. Alternatively you could find yourself calling a company and speaking to the same receptionist every time. You could try asking that receptionist for a direct line to your prospect so that you don't have to keep taking up their time. The most important thing to remember is to keep looking for opportunities to get that direct line on every call you make.

# The
# "What do I say?"
# Monster

In my experience this is most people's biggest monster by far so let's break the question down. When you make your calls you need to know that you are going to be speaking to two very different kinds of people — **gatekeepers** and **key decision makers** (KDM's). In this section we will look at how those roles are different and how best to communicate effectively with each.

# The gatekeeper

Gatekeepers are the people who decide whether or not you will get through to the prospects you need to talk to.

Anyone who picks up a phone in a business you are calling could potentially be a gatekeeper. This could just be someone who happened to walk past the phone when it rang. Those types of unexpecting gatekeepers might put you through straight away but they could also be nervous or new to the business and ask you to call back. You may get lucky and find yourself talking directly to your prospect on the first call but unless you called their direct line or their mobile number this doesn't tend to happen that often.

Whoever answers, always be polite. I have had conversations in the past with people who claimed not to know where the boss was or when they would return, who later turned out to actually be the boss just trying to find out the nature of the call.

The most likely person to answer however, will probably be a switchboard operator and/or a PA. These are experienced gatekeepers who have learned many different ways to get rid of unprepared cold callers. In the table below you can see the kind of responses you can expect if you call without having done any research or at least attempted to make contact by direct mail or GDPR compliant email.

| They will ask | You will say | They will respond | Result |
|---|---|---|---|
| Do you have a name? | ...No | I'm sorry we have a no name policy. | End of call. |
| Is he/she expecting your call? | ...No | The best thing to do is send an email. | Get generic info@company.com email |
| Have you spoken to them before? | ...No | I'm sorry we don't take unsolicited calls. | End of call. |
| Is this a sales call? | ...Erm | I'm sorry we don't take sales calls. | End of call. |

As you can see there, if you don't have a name and haven't made contact before you will most likely have a very short call or be asked to send an email to a generic info@ or enquiries@ address which will, most likely, go straight to their junk mail folder and never be seen again.

The first two questions **"Do you have a name?"** and **"Is he/she expecting your call?"** can be taken care of quite simply. If you can ask for someone by name and you have at least tried to send that person some kind of communication (direct mail, social media or GDPR compliant email) in which you explained that you will be calling them in the next few days, then you shouldn't have any trouble getting past that point. You will have started the conversation by asking for a specific person and said that you are following up on an email/direct mail.

The next two questions **"Have you spoken to them before?"** and **"Is this a sales call?"** are trickier. You can choose to either flat out lie with all the risks that may involve, or you can present yourself in such a way that you never get asked those questions in the first place (hint: this is a much better option). Bear in mind that if you lie you could well find yourself facing an angry prospect who will not only end the call but may then also be irritated enough to make sure any further calls from you are automatically blocked.

So how do you ensure you don't get asked tricky questions like this? The answer is to **try to see cold calls from the gatekeeper's point of view**. A lot of people treat cold calling as though it were a battle with gatekeepers to defeat, assets to seize and key decision makers to overwhelm until they give up and let you in, but that is part of why so many telemarketing campaigns fail, or produce worthless leads. Cold calling shouldn't be a violent, take no prisoners gladiatorial fight to the death. It works much better as a dance where, if you know the steps, both you and your prospects can actually enjoy the interaction. The key is to listen, be as charming as possible and use your natural senses of empathy and understanding to align your prospect's needs to your own. These are qualities rarely found at the other end of a cold call. If you use them well, you will have a huge advantage over any thoughtless, cold calling drone who is all about battles, rigid scripts and winning at all costs.

## The gatekeeper's challenge

All gatekeepers have to strike a tricky balance between the need to put important people through (a potentially huge client, the boss's wife etc.) while at the same time stopping sales calls. If they are rude to someone important they could get in trouble but **they can't ask the one question that would make their job much simpler**.

The question is:

# "Are you important?"

As a result they have to look for any clues they can in order to try and guess a caller's status. This could be the way a person introduces themselves, their tone, how they refer to their company and many other things.

Here are some examples and assumptions a gatekeeper might make based on how you introduce yourself:

| How you introduce yourself | What the gatekeeper might then assume | What the gatekeeper might decide to do next |
| --- | --- | --- |
| Hi... John please. | Caller is important, must know John and is in a hurry. | Ask who's calling and put them through. Note: only effective with small businesses. |
| Hi... John Smith please. | Caller may know John. Has called here before. | Ask who's calling and what the call's regarding and then put them through. |
| Hi, it's <first name> from <company name>. Can I speak to John Smith please. | Caller may have called here before but probably doesn't know John. | Ask what the call's regarding and then if the answer doesn't sound like a sales call put him through. |
| Hi, my name is <full name> and I'm calling from <company name>. Could I please speak with Mr Smith? | Caller doesn't know Mr Smith. It is very likely this is a sales call. | Ask what the call's regarding and then ask Mr Smith if he wants to take a sales call. |
| Hello Sir/Madam, my name is <full name> from <company name>. How are you today? | This is a sales call! | End the call as fast as possible and also possibly block future calls from that number. |

By the way, did you notice that the first three options in this table end with a full stop while the last two end with question marks? This is not an accident. When someone asks a question the pitch of their voice tends to go up at the end of the sentence. Most people do this unconsciously and it helps the listener identify that the statement they are hearing is a question. When you are on the phone, if you keep your voice flat at the end you will sound less needy and this will often encourage the gatekeeper to interrogate you less. If you're not used to doing this it may feel strange and counter-intuitive. You may also feel it's rude but remember you're trying to influence someone's behaviour and it is because people don't speak this way normally that this technique can be very effective. Try asking some flat questions now and compare them to how you would normally speak. Get others to listen to you and give you feedback.

Coming back to the options in the table, the one I would recommend for most situations is the second one: **"Hi, John Smith please."** It gives just enough of a suggestion that you are familiar with the prospect and have called before, without being pushy and it works well with most types of businesses. It may feel counter-intuitive but the less information you provide to a gatekeeper (at least initially) the better. You should always have an answer ready if they ask you a question but remember that the less you say the more they will have to assume which is better for you.

# The key decision maker (KDM)

In the previous section we looked at what to say to gatekeepers and how to manage your interactions with them effectively. The result of following these steps is that gatekeepers will then start to put you through to KDM's rather than turn you away, but how do you make sure you are talking to a genuine KDM and not just another gatekeeper?

A great **KDM** is someone who...

- is at the right executive level in a business that requires your type of offering.
- is in the right size of business or organisation to be of value to you.
- is empowered to commission your services or buy your product.
- is in a buying cycle, meaning that they are in the process of looking for new suppliers or are reviewing their budgets.

Usually the higher you go in an organisation the more decision making gets done. There are exceptions though. Sometimes you may find yourself having a great conversation with the chairman of a business only to discover at the end that they are semi-retired and don't really have much input into the business (which is now being run by their son for example). You may also find yourself talking to the Managing

Director of a branch office who can't actually make decisions without board level approval from head office. Issues like this are part of the reason research done before calling begins will save so much time further down the line.

Either way, once a gatekeeper has put you through to the person you are trying to reach, you will now face the "What do I say?" monster again but at a higher level and your approach will need to be different. Fortunately there is a simple tool that can be adapted to any business and which makes this challenge much easier to deal with. It is called the **direct value statement** and is one of the most important elements of any successful telemarketing campaign.

# The direct value statement (DVS)

**Eight seconds** doesn't sound that long but that's about the length of time a **key decision maker** will give you when you're cold calling a business. If you succeed, it will buy you another thirty seconds of their time and then you can continue to build their interest to the point where they will, hopefully, agree to a meeting.

So how do you summarise your business and what you have to offer in eight seconds?

The **Direct Value Statement** (or DVS) is an extremely effective way of doing that. It takes the form of a couple of sentences which are designed to establish your value

**immediately** at the start of a call. It is most effective when it doesn't contain any marketing speak, business jargon or clichés such as "We pride ourselves on really looking after our customers". It also definitely can't include phrases like "How are you today?"...

The following (somewhat tongue in cheek) example demonstrates the basic structure of a DVS:

**Hi, it's Bob calling from Free Trousers For Ever.
We're a company who specialise in providing you
with free trousers for the rest of your life.
Have you thought of the benefits of never
having to pay for trousers again?**

Straight away you're saying "Hey, if you keep talking to me you'll get free trousers". You're then following up with an open question designed so that a yes or no answer won't end the conversation and will, hopefully, encourage more discussion.

Some people will never want free trousers and some will reject any approach out of hand. This is sometimes because, amongst other things, they've probably recently had to endure hundreds of badly planned marketing calls of the "How are you today?" variety. If you come across someone like that just ask them if they would be happy to receive some information by email and move on. The great thing is that the people who are left know what you're offering. You **valued their time** and people really appreciate that. I've heard some people say you should treat every call you make like the most important call your prospects will ever receive but no one is going to think your call is valuable unless you can convince them it is… and quickly!

I tend to start my DVS's with:

**"Hi, It's Orion from Abbot-Davies Associates. We're a company who specialise in…"**

Saying you specialise is important because you're telling them you're an expert at the thing you do. People like experts and always seem to respond that much better than if you reel off a huge list of areas that you cover.

So how do you make your own DVS?

# The 2 bucket method

Imagine you have two buckets. In one of them you put all the words that describe what people LOVE about having goods and services provided by your business and also the words they used to describe what they loved about dealing with you personally. Recommendations people have written for you are an excellent place to look for these words. If you don't have any written recommendations yet you could ask previous clients, colleagues or other acquaintances who have been delighted by your work, to describe how it felt to have you solve their problem and help their businesses grow.

Take a look at this word cloud:

Do some of these words describe how your clients have felt about you and the work you have done for them?

In the second bucket you put all the words that describe what people FEAR about the risks associated with doing business with your type of company. This doesn't mean you or your company personally but rather what people might fear about using your kind of services or products. Do the words below sound familiar?

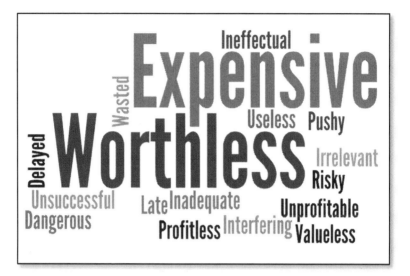

Now all you do is say "Hi, It's <first name> from <company name>. We're a company who specialise in <one thing people love about what your business does> without causing <a thing people fear>".

Try a few combinations using the words in your bucket and you should find one that sounds right for your business and fits your purposes well. Remember that the sooner you establish your value the better. Also, If your company name includes a description of what you do, like Free Trousers For Ever (or say… EasyJet, PayPal, Facebook etc.) that's ideal. Remember you're always trying to get across what you're offering and what your value is as quickly and efficiently as possible.

Here are a few examples of how you might structure DVS's from the words in your LOVE and FEAR buckets:

| LOVE | FEAR | We're a company who specialise in... |
|------|------|-------------------------------------|
| Reliable | Expensive | Reliable Business IT support with low fixed monthly fees. |
| Fast | Risky | Same day food delivery for your staff, at their desks with no upfront costs. |
| Patient | Useless | Taking all the time you need to organise the perfect team building getaway. |
| Effective | Worthless | Effective health and safety training that will protect your staff and your business. |

There is an art to putting together a great DVS and when it happens you will know it straight away because it sounds right. Also there is no rule that says you can't start with the FEAR and move on to the LOVE.

It's whatever gets your message across in the best way possible that still sounds natural. Bear in mind that you will probably have to say this phrase hundreds of times so the less it sounds like a sales pitch the easier that will be for you to do.

# Appeal to the gut

A good DVS will usually strike an emotional cord which is why it is based on LOVE and FEAR.

As Robert Keith Leavitt put it:

**"People don't ask for facts in making up their minds. They would rather have one good soul-satisfying emotion than a dozen facts."**

Some might think that it would be better to take all the time you need to carefully explain all the facts, figures and technological details to your prospects as soon as possible. The idea being that they will understand your offering better and be more qualified as a result. There are several problems with this approach.

Although a prospect will almost certainly want to hear as much detail as possible about your offering during a face to face meeting, things are very different on your first cold call with them. You don't yet have their interest so you need to **appeal to their gut**. During any kind of first contact, including when receiving B2B cold calls, most people tend to listen with their gut first and their brains second. This is why the Direct Value Statement is structured around emotions such as love and fear.

B2B cold calling is also about getting a foot in the door as quickly and efficiently as possible and securing that meeting for your client or yourself. Once you, or they, are in the door the chances of a successful outcome increase dramatically. As one of the most successful sales people I ever knew once said to me, **"Just get me in there face to face, talking to the right person, with the right budget and I'll turn them into a customer."** As a B2B telemarketer, once you've got them or yourself a physical meeting with the right prospect, you've done your job.

You will also generally struggle to find anyone willing to listen to lots of facts or answer lots of questions during a cold call. Even telemarketing survey campaigns have to bear this in mind. Once you actually get through to them most people, if they're feeling cooperative, may answer three or four quick questions before ending the call. In fact you can often hear a prospect's interest diminishing with each new question! This is why it is so important to ask as few questions as possible while making sure those questions are encouraging them to talk.

# Open vs. closed questions

You've seen a few examples of some open questions to follow up with after your DVS but why are they so important? The reason is that open questions encourage more discussion whereas closed ones limit your options. Take a look at the following table for some examples of closed questions and the kind of outcome you might expect if you ask them.

| Closed questions | Response | Outcome |
| --- | --- | --- |
| Have you got a second for a quick chat? | No | End of call |
| Do you need our services? | No | |
| Are you looking for a new supplier? | No | |
| Would you like to take part in our survey? | No | |
| Are you happy with your current provider? | Yes | |

If you ask an open question you are encouraging more discussion and not giving your prospect an easy way to get rid of you. Take a look at the following table to see examples of how open questions can really help to keep the conversation going. It is worth noting that open questions don't prevent yes or no answers. They just encourage people to answer you in a way that won't end the call.

| Open questions | Response | Outcome |
|---|---|---|
| Did you receive the email I sent you? | Yes | You can now discuss the email. |
| | No | You can offer to resend it. |
| Have you reviewed the services you use recently? | Yes | You can ask what "pain points" they discovered. |
| | No | You can pitch your DVS. |
| Have you taken part in our survey before? | Yes | You can discuss their experience of the last survey and offer to update their answers. |
| | No | You can discuss the survey. |
| Is there anything about your current provider that you wish worked better? | Yes | You can ask them what could be improved. |
| | No | People rarely say no to this question but if they do you can ask them about an aspect of their services that is unlikely to work perfectly. Could it be cheaper, faster or better quality? |

Take a moment now to think about some open questions that relate to your offering. Try starting with:

**Have you considered the impact of...?**
**Have you thought about what you could do with...?**
**What would be the most...?**
**Have you looked at how...?**

Then follow this by describing an obvious benefit for your prospect. Once you have thought of a few of these questions try them out and see the effect they have on the conversation.

Below are a couple of DVS's together with their corresponding open questions:

Hi, It's <first name> from <company name>. I understand you recently visited our bankruptcy advice page. We're a company who specialise in getting businesses back to healthy finance levels within three to six weeks. **Open Question >** What aspect of your business do you think is causing the most issues?

Hi, It's <first name> from <company name>. We're a company who specialise in halving your social media marketing costs while doubling the profit you make from it. **Open Question >** Have you considered how much profit you could be making from an efficient social media strategy?

# Time for your next story...
# A true friend

**Uo was a large male Humpback whale** with a problem. He had eaten his fill of delicious food swarms in the Sea of Ice Giants some time ago and had decided it was time to swim to warmer climes and find a mate. The problem was that, in his excitement at the prospect of starting a family, he swam a little too fast and arrived in the waters around the Land Above the World too early. There was not as much food here and few others of his kind to hear his song. There was nothing much to do and he was bored. He spent some of his time looking for the boats that would come from the island every so often. When he found one he would swim up to it and breathe out noisily. He could hear happy sounds when he did it and the more he kept doing it, the more boats seemed to come. A few times he even jumped out of the world in front of them and they always seemed to make more happy sounds when he splashed down. It wasn't enough though and he was soon feeling even more fed up and also quite lonely.

It wasn't that he was alone mind you. That would have actually been easier. It was more that in these waters those who kept talking to him were not of his kind and were also quite annoying. They would come up to him every day by the dozen, shouting their messages at him.

"Food swarms! We can get you food swarms! Come and get your food swarms! The best food swarms anywhere!"

"Need to clean that rough skin? We know the best rock beds! Give us your moulting business!"

"Get the latest songs here! The best songs to sing! Everyone will love your songs!"

He didn't need food swarms because he had eaten so much before coming and didn't need to clean his skin either, but they wouldn't shut up. He also didn't have any problems with his songs, which he had been singing all his life. While all these annoying ones would pester him, he did notice one silvery swimmer would often stay around him and just keep him company silently. It was a little strange, but it didn't seem to want anything from him, so he just ignored it. One day after a few weeks the silvery one came to him and said hello. Uo greeted him back and asked what he wanted. The silvery one paused thoughtfully and said:

"My name is Onasai. Please forgive my presumption but you seem lonely. I noticed you arrived before the other ones of your kind some time ago and I was wondering if that was causing you some problems. Well, there's no need to worry because I specialise in helping those who are lonely". Uo asked Onasai how he could possibly help him and Onasai replied, "I spoke to a large and very attractive one of your kind who arrived a few days ago. I saw her on the other side of the island of the above worlders and she told me she is also looking for a mate. If you have time I would be happy to find her for you and arrange a meeting?"

Uo felt a swell of excitement for the first time in a while. He was so grateful that Onasai had noticed what he really needed and agreed for a meeting to take place as soon as possible. In return he told Onasai where he had seen all the above worlders who had nets to catch his kind so that he would be safe. Uo was soon introduced to a beautiful whale named Tatala. They fell for each other immediately and, before long, they too had a little family of their own.

I hope you enjoyed Uo's story. **Uo** means friend in Samoan because the people we call are not the enemy. **Onasai** means patient, this is a quality that I must admit I had to work on for some time when I started my own telemarketing journey many years ago. I chose **Tatala** which means open because being a friend who is patient and open is a great way to approach your calling.

# Putting it all together:

Now that we have looked at the various responses that interacting with **gatekeepers** and **key decision makers** produce, we can put these elements together to see how a typical conversation would flow. Following that, we will then examine each part and look in more depth at how these strategies work.

Let's first look at the flow of a typical successful call:

**Caller**: Hi, John Smith please.

**Gatekeeper**: Who's calling please?

**Caller**: It's Jack from Awesome Widgets.

**Gatekeeper**: Can I ask what the call's regarding?

**Caller**: Yes, I'm just following up on a letter we sent him a couple of days ago.

**Gatekeeper**: Ok, I'll just put you through.

(pause)

**KDM**: Hello?

**Caller**: Hi, is this John?

**KDM**: Yes.

**Caller**: Hi it's Jack from Awesome Widgets? I'm just following up on a letter we sent you a couple of days ago? Did you receive something from us?

**KDM**: Erm... sorry I don't think so. Can you tell me what this is about?

**Caller**: Sure, so we're a company who specialise in awesome widgets that remove the need to have expensive thingamajigs and typically increase your profit margins by over seventy-five percent. Have you reviewed your thingamajigs recently?

**KDM**: Not really but it's something that's been on our radar for a while. Our thingamajigs were part of one of the companies that we took over a few years ago and there just hasn't been time to look at that yet. We did look at some widgets last year but they seemed expensive and we just weren't sure they would help solve the thingamajig issues we were having. Your timing's pretty good actually cos we're about to look at our budgets for the rest of the quarter...

**Caller**: Ok, well what I'd like to do is send you a one-pager that explains what we do in more detail... Would that be alright?

**KDM**: Sure, could you send it to John Smith at

doohickey.com?

**Caller**: ok... and then maybe we could pop in for a chat in the next couple of weeks to go through it with you? Do you have some time in the next couple of weeks where we could meet up?

**KDM**: Could we make it for the beginning of next month as we will have sorted our budgets by then?

**Caller**: Sure, so how would Thursday the seventh at twelve o'clock be for you?

**KDM**: Erm..... (pause while he looks at diary) Sure, can You send me a meeting request?

**Caller**: Absolutely.

Then you would finish by confirming (whenever possible) any other useful information such as:

- Their address, direct lines, mobile numbers.
- Who will be at to the meeting (just them or other managers).
- Any specific questions the KDM would like you to have answers for, ahead of the meeting.

Now let's go back through that conversation and not only look at its parts but also explore some of the alternative paths the conversation could follow.

**Caller**: Hi, John Smith please.

**Gatekeeper**: Who's calling please?

**Caller**: It's <first name> from <company name>.

**Gatekeeper**: Can I ask what the call's regarding?

**Caller**: Yes, I'm just following up on <an email> / <a letter> we sent him a couple of days ago.

I find that, at this point, most gatekeepers will put you through because you:

- Asked for the KDM by name.
- Sounded like you may have called before and may know the KDM.
- Sounded like people should recognise your voice already because you didn't give out your name until asked.
- Said that you had already communicated by email or post with the KDM.

Essentially, you have preemptively removed a lot of the gatekeepers objections and most of them will just put you through at this point. You may find that they put you through to another gatekeeper like a personal assistant for example but then you would just repeat what you said to the first gatekeeper.

Some gatekeepers may want to know a little more and will ask:

**Gatekeeper**: Could you tell me what this is about please?

**Caller**: Sure, we're a <**BRIEF** company description such as Mortgage Broker, HR Specialist company, Health & Safety organisation>. I'm just trying to find out if John's received our email / letter.

At this point about half of the remaining gatekeepers will put you through. The rest may ask you to:

- Resend your email or post
- Call back
- Wait for a response

So long as they don't flat out ask you not to call again, you would just mark them as a "Callback" and choose an appropriate time and date to have another go.

However, the more likely outcome, is that they will put you through to the KDM. Below is a typical example of that interaction:

**KDM**: Hello?

**Caller**: Hi, is this John?

**KDM**: Yes.

**Caller**: Hi it's <first name> from <company name>, I'm just following up on an email / letter that we sent you a couple of days ago? Did you receive something from us?

**KDM**: Erm… sorry I don't think so. Can you tell me what this is about?

**Note**: The interaction above may seem unnecessary or even trivial but it is actually very important because it avoids having to go straight into your pitch. It makes your interaction more like a conversation and encourages the KDM to ask what the call is about. After that it's a lot more acceptable if what you say sounds like a pitch because they are the ones who asked for it. Now you are free to go on to your **Direct Value Statement (DVS)**:

Sure, so we're a company who specialise in **<one thing people love about what your business does>** without causing **<a thing people fear>**.

Open question:

Have you considered / thought about / looked at…

What you want at this point is for the KDM to talk as much as possible in response to your open question. The more the better because that signals that they are willing to engage with you and have decided that it's ok to spend time talking to you. You should never interrupt them or ask too many questions if they are enjoying giving you lots of information. If you don't understand what they are saying just pretend that you do and look it up later!

I remember once, after weeks of carefully nurturing a gatekeeper, I was put through to the Head of Marketing for EMEA (Europe, the Middle East and Africa) for a multi-billion-dollar telecom company. Once I had introduced myself and gone through my **Direct Value Statement** and **Open Question**, he was very happy to talk at length about their pain points and issues in a very technically complex way.

He talked for about twenty minutes and I understood about fifty percent of the technical terms he used. I wasn't going to stop him and ask for clarifications every time I didn't understand something. Instead, I just said "Uh huh..." as knowledgably as I possibly could. Once the call was over, I went through my notes and researched everything he said until I could make sense of it. The prize at the end of that conversation was that he agreed to a very valuable face to face meeting with my client.

As a general rule, nothing in your conversation with a KDM should cause them to repeat themselves or otherwise experience unnecessary stress. If you make the experience of talking to you a pleasant one, where the KDM can clearly see the value of talking to you and doesn't feel like you have wasted any time getting to the point, they will be far more willing to open their diary and agree to a time and date for a meeting.

**Offer to send them something:**

"...Ok, well what I'd like to do is send you a one-pager that explains what we do in more detail, Is that ok?"

You should always have a follow up email, ready to send to a prospect, the moment they ask for it. They won't remember your call for very long, so you need to be quick. This should be a simple introductory email reminding your prospect about your conversation and including a one-pager document, ideally in the form of a small pdf attachment. It needs to be small (ideally under one megabyte) as large attachments often trigger spam filters and your email might not get through.

Here is an example of an email you might send to someone who could not talk on the phone but asked for more info:

---

Hi <Prospect's first name>,

Thank you for taking my call today.

Please find attached the information we discussed. As per our conversation I will call you on Wednesday at 3:00 pm to talk through this in more detail.

Kind regards,

<Your first name>
<Email signature with your contact details>

---

The brilliant thing about offering to send them something by email is that almost everyone says yes. This is because some of them will genuinely want more information and the rest think you're about to go away.

**The point is to get them to agree to something.**

Experience shows that if a **KDM** says "Yes" to something, the probability that they will say "Yes" to the **next thing they are asked** increases dramatically. In other words, once you have managed to get them to come out of their often default mental state of resisting any kind of sales call, it's far more likely they will respond positively to whatever you do next.

And here's what you do next…

Ask them if the email you have for them is correct.

"I've got john.smith@doohickey.com is that correct?"

**Top tip**: It's far less off-putting to ask a **KDM** prospect to correct an email you already have than to ask them to supply one from scratch. Also, if you told them at the start of the call that you were just following up on an email you sent them, it would be strange to not have one, even if it's wrong. Once they confirm their correct **direct** email and depending on their level of interest during the call, you could then quickly say:

"…and then maybe **follow up with a call** to go through it in more detail…"

Do you remember the open questions we looked at earlier? The point of those questions was partly to get information but much more importantly it was to get your prospects talking so you could gauge their level of interest. If they were **very** interested, such as in the successful call example we looked at before, you could say instead:

"...and then maybe **pop in for a chat** to go through it with you in more detail."

**Top tip**: Many of the key words used throughout these example conversations sound like they were just thought up on the spur of the moment.

Phrases such as:

- "**Just following up**"
- "We're a company who **specialise** in"
- "I'd like to send you **one-pager**"
- "Maybe **pop in** for a chat"

These sound casual, relaxed and spontaneous but they are not being used accidentally. All of these phrases are designed to have a specific effect. They can be used to encourage interest or to make you sound less like a salesperson. For example, when you tell someone that you "specialise" in solving the type of problem they have, it increases their confidence in you. They also help to make sure that what you are saying won't make the **key decision maker** anxious. You could, of course say, "Can I send you an email?" or "Can I meet up with you?" but it's a lot less threatening to say, "I'd like to send you one-pager" or "Maybe pop in for a chat".

Once they have agreed to a meeting or follow up call you should always **offer** a date and time. If you ask them when they are free you're putting responsibility on them and making them do the work which can make talking to you a less pleasant experience. One of the golden rules I tend to follow with cold calling is:

**"Make the gatekeeper do all the work and the key decision maker none."**

As we saw before, with gatekeepers you should never volunteer any information that isn't explicitly requested because you want them to have to guess your status and make assumptions about your level of importance. The opposite is true with key decision makers as you are trying to make sure that talking to you is an effortless and valuable experience for them.

I remember once I had to nurture a KDM over several months before they decided to agree to a meeting. When they finally agreed they told me they enjoyed talking to me so much more than other telemarketers because, as they put it "it always feels like I'm sitting back and having my tummy tickled." I took that as a compliment!

# Let's do it!

At this point you may still be feeling quite nervous about making that first call, particularly if you haven't done a lot of cold calling in the past. Bear in mind that your first few calls are probably going to be a little wobbly. The thing to remember is that it doesn't matter if things don't work out at first. Don't worry about messing up. There will always be more people to call and, unless you said something particularly memorable, your call will be forgotten almost instantly. So long as you keep paying attention to the information coming your way, new opportunities will always present themselves.

When a call doesn't go well, give yourself a moment to think about what happened and see if you notice anything about it that could be useful for the next one.

As the saying goes:

**"Whenever you fall, pick something up." — Oswald Avery**

An unsuccessful call almost always leaves a trail of breadcrumbs that could give you clues about how to make the next call better.

For example, imagine a call where you are told no one wants to talk to you because the company is doing its yearly accounts and is snowed under. You could check the calendar and see if it is time for most companies to do the same (often this happens around March/April). If it is, then on the next call to a similar company you make sure to ask for someone who is still potentially a good prospect for you but has as little to do with finance as possible. When you get through you say:

**"Hi, I know you're probably busy with your year-end accounts at the moment so I don't want to take up any of your time. We're a company who <insert DVS>. What I'd like to do is send you a one-pager that talks about what we do in more detail and maybe catch up after the account submission date?"**

Instead of being told no one is available you may now have someone who:

- Has agreed to receive some information.
- Has confirmed their personal email address.
- Has given you their direct line.
- Is expecting a call from you in a few weeks/months.


Being able to dynamically adapt your strategy based on real time feedback is one way to make sure that every call you make, including those that don't seem to go well, are in some way useful to you.

When I use this approach I often find that the call back I make after their busy period is almost a warm call. We can share a laugh and bond over what a crazy time it was for them. They may even volunteer anecdotes about their experiences. So long as they are the right person to talk to, any form of bonding is going to make future conversations easier.

It's important to say at this point that I'm not suggesting you pretend to be their friend here. It may look like we are treading a fine line between **honesty** and **authenticity** but I believe it is not only possible but in fact necessary to be authentic. All of these attempts at bonding are simply to lower your threat level and help them realise that you are different to the other telemarketers they have spoken to. By not treating gatekeepers and key decision makers like the enemy you are encouraging them not to treat you like the enemy either.

# How do I close?

One of the things that sometimes gets lost in the process of B2B cold calling is unfortunately also one of the most important.

A trap I used to fall into when I first started calling was that I would be so relieved to have got through to the right person and that they were responding positively that I would hesitate to "close" (in B2B cold calling terms this refers to successfully booking an appointment as **that is the ultimate goal**). I would end the call with an agreement to call at a later date to discuss my offering further and often miss the fact that the prospect could well have been ready there and then to agree to a meeting.

A useful way to look at closing is to imagine you have a descending scale of potential positive outcomes. To use your listening skills, your intelligence, your empathy and understanding to nurture a prospect is great but front of mind should always be the question:

**"Is there an opportunity here for me to close right now?"**

An ideal prospect should close easily and quickly. They will agree to a face to face meeting at their offices at a specific time and date within the next four weeks. They will also happily confirm their direct email address, their direct line and the address of the meeting and accept your emailed meeting request the moment they receive it.

If they don't want a meeting then you just go for the next best thing on the descending scale.

- Will they agree to a conference call at a specific time and date within the next four weeks?
  No? Then…

- Will they confirm their direct email address and their direct line?
  No? Then…

- Will they agree to receiving some more information by email and a call in a few months?

The key is to keep in focus what you are trying to achieve by the end of every call. Try to keep your goals in mind all the time and a sharp eye on any opportunity to close.

# Don't always assume you're the problem

Back when I was just a little baby telemarketer in knee-high socks, I thought that if I didn't get someone to agree to a meeting or a further call immediately, it was because I had somehow failed to impress them with my offering. While that can definitely sometimes be the case, you should leave a little room for the possibility that it might not have anything to do with you. There could be any number of reasons that a prospect may not want to admit the real reason they aren't taking the call further. Some examples from my own experience have included:

- The company was going bust.
- The prospect recently handed in their notice but could not discuss it.
- They were being acquired by another company and didn't know if they would still have a job.
- They were being investigated for fraud, health and safety issues, malpractice etc...
- The MD had just been diagnosed with a terminal illness but not gone public yet.
- The person I needed to talk to had just been fired and his (now ex) PA could not discuss it.

This also applies if a previously **warm** contact who had agreed to a meeting in principle suddenly starts backing off and won't agree to any further meetings or calls. In one case I had been working on for some weeks, the prospect was about to agree to a meeting when an existing supplier of theirs heard they were thinking of switching to someone else and threatened to take them to court for breaking their contract.

Keep in mind that everyone you speak to has their own story and that it affects every part of their decision making process. If you sense an unusual resistance and the person you are speaking to seems open to it, you could try to have a conversation about what the issue may be. Always be respectful, though, as they will not thank you for adding to their problems.

I remember a call with a very friendly prospect who was very positive and very interested in the service I was discussing with him. He said he was happy to arrange a meeting but asked me to wait a couple of months as he was going into hospital because "the doctors seemed to have found a lump" and then he was going on holiday. I called back a few months later and when I asked to speak to him there was a shuffling around of phones and a pause. A disconcerted PA then spoke to me and said that sadly he had passed away. She didn't say what form of cancer it was but I can tell you I spent a few sleepless nights after that worrying about my own mortality. After that I never forgot that there could be any number of factors behind someone's decision making process and to commit myself to not take things personally.

# Beware the runaway train effect

After a few calls that haven't produced anything of great value or have been met with some hostility there can be a tendency to speed up. Much of the work we do is results driven so a natural response to a lack of results is to speed up. This is a mistake. The faster you talk, the more you sound like a salesperson and it tends to either put people on edge or make them go into a kind of autopilot rejection mode.

If you start to feel the runaway train effect happening **you need to put the brakes on**. For example, you could deliberately pause after they have answered the call and said their introduction; just long enough for them to start to wonder if there is anyone there. This helps you slow down and can have the added benefit of breaking them out of their script. They will then have to improvise and this could result in a much more genuine conversation. Sometimes though they will resent that and try to speed you up by speeding up themselves. Another reason they might be speeding you up by talking fast is that they probably also have to get through a lot of calls. In either situation two runaway trains meeting isn't a good thing. If you can control the pace of the conversation you will greatly increase your chances of getting through to your prospects.

Try the following exercise the next time you are having a conversation. As you are talking and listening in turn, focus on the pace of the conversation. Who is driving it? Is it you or the other person? Is it fast or slow? If you wanted to, could you speed the rate of conversation up or slow it down without the other person noticing? When you speak faster for example, does the other person speed up as well? We are not normally that conscious of this sort of thing in regular conversations. It is pretty clear, though, that it plays a very important role in how people react to what you're saying and even how happy they feel to keep talking to you.

Personally, I tend to speed up a little too much at times after a large amount of calls. When that happens I try to think back to an experiment that I tried with a colleague some time ago. I asked them to listen to me talking as I read out a piece of text from a book. I told them that I would slow down more and more and asked them to tell me when it felt like I was speaking too slowly. I was amazed at how slow I could go before they said it was too much. Try this yourself with a friend. It's an eye opener and it will definitely help you feel more confident to speak slowly and clearly rather than "rush to get it over with".

# The overzealous gatekeeper

Sometimes a gatekeeper will actually be a lot more aggressive than the person you are trying to get through to. This could be because they let someone through previously who they shouldn't have and got told off so now they are overcompensating. It's almost as though they are saying to their boss, "I'll show him how good I am at not letting people through!" If you do then somehow manage to get through, their boss is as nice as pie. They've completely forgotten about the telling off they gave their poor receptionist last week and have no idea she is now blocking ninety-nine percent of their calls regardless of their importance.

One of the other reasons a gatekeeper may be overly aggressive is because they know their boss is unable to say no to people on the phone. This puts them in a strange sort of defensive position because they may feel, in a sense, that they are protecting the company from itself. The best thing to do in this situation is to try to find ways to reassure them or, if all else fails, bypass them by acquiring a direct phone number, for example, or calling at five pm when the boss may be the only one in the office.

# Practice a perfect call

If you make too many calls that don't get through to a prospect it can come as quite a shock when you do suddenly get through. Unfortunately that shock is often noticeable on the other end of the line if it catches you off guard. You may sound surprised, unprepared or confused. A good technique to avoid this is to make a pretend call and imagine your prospect says all the right things so that you are able to go through your entire conversational journey. You should do this every dozen or so calls if you aren't getting through to anyone. This will help you reset your focus and avoid you getting stuck in a downward spiral.

# The power of the pause

When a gatekeeper asks "who is calling?" tell them your first name, then after a pause say "Oh… from" and tell them your company name almost as though it was an afterthought. This suggests that you're even more likely to know the prospect and just remembered that the gatekeeper might need your company name for their notes.

# It's not urgent

The most common outcome of a call is probably that your prospect will simply not be available. Just in case you end up speaking to the same gatekeeper on your next call, an interesting way to make yourself more welcome in future calls is to say that your call isn't urgent and that you will call back another time. Very few cold callers in my experience will say that their call isn't urgent. They want everyone to know that their call is the most important call in the world and don't care if nobody agrees. By saying your call isn't urgent you're being disarming and encouraging gatekeepers to not perceive you as just another cold caller.

# Are we playing fair?

This is one of the questions that comes up from time to time in my Conquer the Telephone Monster® workshops. It is quite natural to wonder if all these techniques, tips and tricks we are looking at are "fair play". Are we tricking or manipulating people in a dishonest way? Is it ok to try to influence someone on the phone with the methods described in this book? This is all very "cloak and dagger stuff" isn't it?

My answer to that question is simply to acknowledge that there are strategies in this book that are designed to influence behaviour but not in an ultimately dishonest way. They are all designed to influence the people you speak with so that they give you **their best response**. If you don't try to maximise someone's potential to react positively to you on the phone they will almost certainly react negatively.

**No one is standing by their phone eager to receive the next sales call.**

Every time you get through, you have to deal with whatever damage the hundreds of sales calls before yours may have done. I have had so many conversations with **key decision makers** that have ended with them thanking me for not being pushy and for getting to the point. Often they are surprised that they enjoyed the conversation, but to get to that point, I had to **use every strategy available** to me to encourage them to shake off their natural tendency to reject any kind of sales approach.

Take, for example, the "overzealous gatekeeper" mentioned earlier. On the one hand, you could say that the methods used to influence their decision to put you through to the **key decision maker** seem to operate on an almost unconscious level and that that isn't fair. However, this means that you then end up talking to a **key decision maker** who is delighted that you called and agrees to a meeting that helps both your businesses grow.

Telling someone that your call isn't a "sales call" when it

obviously is or that the **key decision maker** knows you or has spoken to you before when they haven't is dishonest. You will most likely get found out with all the negative consequences that may entail. **Lying is never a good strategy**. What we're talking about in this book is **influencing** decision makers so that they listen to you for long enough to understand the value of your offering.

So long as you genuinely believe (and can demonstrate if needed!) that your offering could be of genuine interest to the person you are having a conversation with, then all these strategies are simply there to help you get your point across in a challenging environment where people tend to reject any sales approach that interrupts their day.

**Note**: The following section delves into **the world of spreadsheets** quite extensively. If you are not overly familiar with Excel and would rather continue focusing on calling strategies, please feel free to skip to the **"How do I stay focused?" Monster** section on page 112. You can then return later when you are in front of your computer and ready to start organising your next successful calling campaign!

# The
# "How do I keep track?"
## Monster

Once you have made a few calls, how do you keep track of
**what happened**, and **what needs to happen next**? If you're
just making a few calls then wouldn't a notepad or even just
some post-it notes be enough? The short answer is no.

The long answer, as anyone who has tried this will

probably tell you, is noooooooooooooooooooo!

For example, let's look at a typical six to eight week tele-marketing campaign, designed with the intention of producing high quality leads in the form of face to face meetings or conference calls. You are going to need somewhere between two to three hundred companies to call to generate between five to ten high quality leads. There are of course many variables that affect your output, but let's assume an average set of circumstance for the sake of argument.

The first day of calling you might make one hundred first contact calls with simple notes that reflect the outcome of each call. The next day you will make fifty first contact calls but then also have to make fifty follow up calls from the previous days' calling. Those notes will need to be added to your original notes so that you can start to build a clear picture of developing interactions with each company you have called. By this stage, notepads or post it notes have long ceased to be of any use other than as confusing clutter on your desk.

This is where Microsoft's **Excel** can be an invaluable tool to help you keep track of everything you do efficiently. Excel is a multi-platform software solution that lets you organise your data in columns and rows that can be sorted and searched and manipulated in any number of ways to present you with the information you need... It can also easily be customised to provide you with your optimal workflow and data management needs depending on whatever you need it to do.

There are many dedicated software solutions out there

that will help you run telemarketing campaigns and they certainly have their strengths but none of them are as universal as Excel. Most people have it already as part of their office subscription and over the last few years it has moved from a purely Windows based platform to being available on Apple's iOS system as well as all the major mobile platforms. Excel is also compatible with most of the top Customer Relationship Management (**CRM**) solutions available. This means these systems can both export and import in Excel format so if a client is using a CRM system to manage their prospect, Excel will easily fit into their processes. Amazingly, at the time of writing this there are reportedly well over a billion users of Excel worldwide!

# Different strokes

Many people use Excel as a database for example, where names or addresses would be separated into columns so that each part could easily be searched and tasks like mail merging could readily be automated. This is where they would typically have separate columns for **Salutation**, **First Name**, **Middle Initial**, **Last Name**, etc. and also where addresses might be segmented into **Address 1**, **Address 2**, **Address 3**, **City**, **County**, **Postcode**, **Country** and so on.

The needs of a B2B Telemarketer are very different though. For us, it's all about **speed and a smooth uninterrupted workflow**. Most often, we only have seconds during a call to retrieve certain bits of information. Getting to that information quickly and efficiently is paramount. This is why you won't see segmented names and addresses here. This is also why all the information you have for a company is in one row and the focus is on promoting useful information and demoting (but not deleting) less useful information. We want to pursue the best person within an organisation and call the best number for them and have the best address to ask them for a meeting at with nothing else in the way. Confirming someone's address, whether email or postal should be a simple matter of a glance. Recalling something that was said, even months ago on a previous call to a key decision maker needs to be instant. Nothing should break your flow of thought unnecessarily. Also having rapid access to all this information must apply to every contact you call even if you are calling hundreds of people. In the next section we will look at how to set up an Excel spreadsheet so that it is optimised for fast, efficient and stress free calling.

# Setting the stage

## Font and zoom

Setting Excel up properly at the beginning will really help you get to the information you need fast. If you learn the phrase: **"Arial eight at eighty"** it will help you set up any spreadsheet perfectly.

Once you have loaded Excel, select the whole spreadsheet (shortcut: Ctrl+A)

Set the font to Arial at a size of 8 points.

Set the Zoom level to 80% (slider is in the bottom right hand corner).

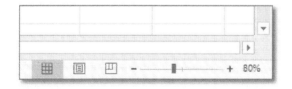

Deselect the rows by clicking in any cell.

This will give you a huge amount of visible data without the need to scroll around.

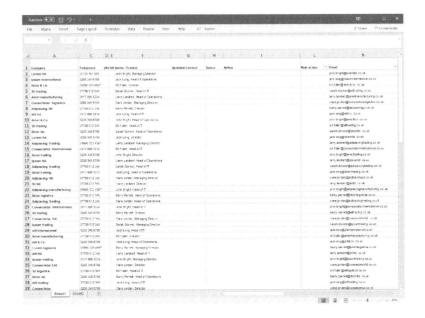

If you have a wide screen monitor, you could easily see the details of over fifty companies at a time and at least twenty columns of separate information about them without having to scroll at all. This is an incredibly useful way of presenting your data, when you often only have seconds to respond to questions, or if you want to quickly confirm an email or postal address.

## Row Height

You may find that the default row height in Excel makes the data feel a little too dense. You can also change the standard row height to 15 except for the top row which you set to 30. To do this you will need to:

Select the whole spreadsheet (shortcut: Ctrl+A).

Right click on any row number label and a menu will appear.

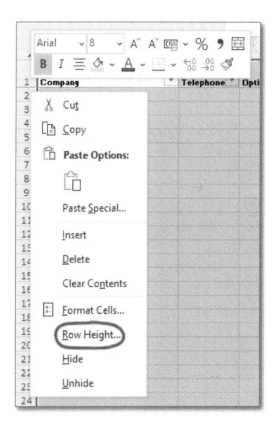

In the menu select "Row Height", enter 15 then click

"OK". Now deselect the rows by clicking in any cell.

Finally select the top row by left clicking on row label number 1.

...and repeat the process above to set the row height to 30. Deselect the rows by clicking in any cell.

You're all set!

# Set up your columns

Use the column headings below to set up your spreadsheet (or download the resource pack spreadsheet template from: abbot-davies.com/resource-pack).

| Col | Column heading | Function |
| --- | --- | --- |
| A | Company | This is for the name of the company, organisation or group you are targeting. If the company changes their name or is acquired by another company you can put the old company name in brackets here to keep a history i.e. "Import Global (was Import UK)" |

| | | |
|---|---|---|
| B | Telephone | This is for the most direct number you have for your prospect regardless of whether it's a landline, mobile or a number with an extension in brackets. Update as required. |
| C | Option | This is where you can make a note of the option sequences you hear when the company you are calling uses an IVR (interactive voice response) system. "Press 3 for Marketing, Press 2 for Product Marketing, Press 4 for EMEA Product Marketing, Thank you, please hold for an assistant" would become: "3,2,4, h" so the next time you call you can save time. It is worth noting that pressing 0 the moment you hear an IVR system begin will often get you straight through to the operator. |
| D | Alt number /extension | Store any other numbers and extensions you have for your contacts in this column. If you start by using a main number but then are given a direct line you would update the "Telephone" column with the direct line and move the old number to this column. This way you are always using the best number you have while never throwing away any of the old numbers in case your main number stops working for some reason. |
| E | Contact | Speed is of the essence so there is no need |

| | name, role | to separate names into different columns for Salutation, First Name, Middle Name, Last Name. Just enter the person's name and role i.e. "John Smith, Director". If their name makes it hard to identify their gender (ex: Charlie, Dannie, Sasha) put Mr or Ms next those first names. Also if the name is pronounced differently to the way it looks put a (pron.) note next to the part that needs it i.e. "Niall (pron. Neil) Smith". |
|---|---|---|
| F | Status | This is a simple one to two word description of the status of your communication with that contact. by using this brief description you can easily sort your data later. See below for some common examples of statuses and descriptions: |

| Status | Describes a prospect who... |
|---|---|
| Callback | is actively being targeted for calling. |
| Lead | has agreed to a meeting or call. |
| Nurture | has shown an interest but isn't ready to agree to a meeting or call yet. |
| Qualified out | is not interested and doesn't want further contact. |
| Email only | will only communicate by |

| | | |
|---|---|---|
| | | email. |
| | | **Long term** may be interested but not in the next six months. |
| G | Notes | This is where you keep track of all interactions with your contacts. For clarity and sorting purposes the last interaction always appears at the start of the note and begins with the date of your interaction followed by a colon. This date is in a reverse format (ex: 20140317) which may seem strange to begin with but is actually very useful for clarity and sorting later on. So for example October 12th 2015 would become 20151012. If you rang a contact who was unavailable on the 5th of July 2017, your note should read: 20170705: Unavailable<br>If you rang that person 2 days later and got their voicemail the whole note would look like: 20170707: Voicemail 20170705: Unavailable<br>(see "The final touches" section below for more details) |
| H | Note updates | This column has the same data validation settings (see next section "Create some drop down menus" for details) as the "Notes" column. It is used to select and customise notes which are then copied over to the front of the cell contents in the Notes column. |

| I | Next action | Here you can make a specific short note about any next action required. It is separate from the status and note column so that it can easily be filtered. It could be as simple as "Send Email" so that you could filter to show all contacts from that days calling who need to be sent an email. Alternatively if you needed to call someone back on a certain date you could put "Callback on 20170711". When you filter this column Excel will automatically sort these dates so you can easily filter out contacts who should not be called before a certain date. |
|---|---|---|
| J | Of note | Put today's date (ex: 20170302) here for any call that was of interest for any reason. This way you can go back and see any calls of note for any days calling. |
| K | Email | The contact's email address. |
| L | Address | The contact's postal address in a single, comma separated line. |
| M | Website | The contact's website. |

# Create some drop down menus

This next section may seem a little more complicated but if you follow the steps you shouldn't have any trouble. Also, as mentioned earlier, you can download a readymade version of the spreadsheet at abbot-davies.com/resource-pack

Excel has a very useful tool for creating drop down lists from which you can pick often used words or pieces of text to populate your cells. This feature means that any date or commonly used word or phrase can simply be selected from a list.

The steps below will show you how to set up a **data validation** list for a column.

First let's make our list.

- Select a worksheet other than the one where all your calling data is (ex: **Sheet2**) and make sure it is blank.
- Set this sheet up using the same "**Arial eight at eighty**" system that you used to set up your main data sheet earlier.
- In cell **B2** of that sheet enter "**Data Validation**" in bold.
- In **B4** enter the title "**Status**".
- Now in **B5 through to B10** enter "Callback", "Lead", "Nurture", "Qualified out", "Email only", "Long term".

You have now created the list that the data validation

tool will use to make your drop down menu.

It should look like this:

| | A | B |
|---|---|---|
| 1 | | |
| 2 | | **Data Validation** |
| 3 | | |
| 4 | | **Status:** |
| 5 | | Callback |
| 6 | | Lead |
| 7 | | Nurture |
| 8 | | Qualified out |
| 9 | | Email only |
| 10 | | Long term |

Select the first worksheet again (ex: **Sheet1**) and select the "**Status**" column.

**Top tip**: Quickly select whole columns or whole rows in Excel by clicking on a cell in that column or row and pressing **Ctrl+Space** to select the column or **Shift+Space** to select the row.

If you set up the spreadsheet according to the earlier instructions this should be column **F**. On the tool ribbon at the top of the Excel window select "**DATA**" and choose the "**Data Validation**" tool. In the drop down menu that appears select "**Data Validation**". This will open the "**Data Validation**" dialogue window below.

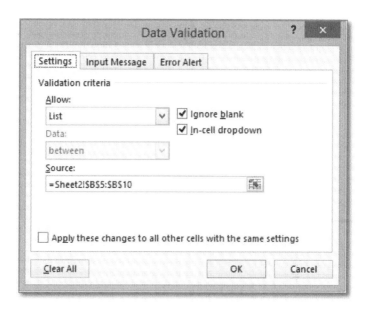

(The keyboard shortcut for this window is **Alt+A,V,V**)

In this window select "**List**" from the "**Allow**" menu. Click on the small "**spreadsheet with a red arrow**" icon  to the right of the "**Source**" window. The "**Data Validation**" dialogue window will be replaced by a thinner window. Select the worksheet where you typed your Data Validation list (**Sheet 2 - B5 through to B10**) and use the mouse to select your status options (Callback, Lead, Nurture, Qualified out, Email only, Long term).

|     | A | B |
| --- | --- | --- |
| 1 |  |  |
| 2 |  | **Data Validation** |
| 3 |  |  |
| 4 |  | **Status:** |
| 5 |  | Callback |
| 6 |  | Lead |
| 7 |  | Nurture |
| 8 |  | Qualified out |
| 9 |  | Email only |
| 10 |  | Long term |

You will notice that a green dotted line appears around your selection and that "=**Sheet2!$B$5:$B$10**" displays in the thin Data Validation window. This represents the location of your status cells so that Excel knows where to look for your list. Now press "**Enter**".

The final step is to select the "**Error Alert**" tab in the "**Data Validation**" dialogue window and **untick** the option titled "**Show error alert after invalid data is entered**". If you don't do this additional step, Excel will give you an error alert if you type anything into a data validation cell that isn't on your list.

Press the "**OK**" button and you will return to the sheet and column you originally selected at the start.

And you're done!

Now, If you select any cell in that column, you will notice a small arrow to the right of the cell. Click on that arrow or with the cell selected press **Alt+(Down arrow)** and your menu will appear. Either select the menu option you want with your arrow keys or click on it to see it copied to your selected cell.

Now you have menus and don't have to type the same words repeatedly as you make your calls.

# Make it stand out

There are occasions when it is useful to have certain words or phrases stand out in your data. The standard procedure for this would be to select your text and change its formatting as needed. If you do this a lot though, it can easily become confusing and unmanageable. It's not uncommon to see businesses using spreadsheets with rows and columns highlighted in bright conflicting colours and find out that no one remembers what most of those coloured sections mean...

Example (using dummy data):

Shocking, isn't it?

Thankfully Excel has a very useful tool called **Conditional Formatting** which allows you to format text based on conditions you set. This is a far more subtle way to highlight important cells, rows and columns than just hosing the sheet down with various colours and hoping for the best.

For example, you could have a cell background turn red when you type the words "invoice overdue" into it.

In the resource pack spreadsheet this function is used to make the words "**Lead**" and "**Nurture**" stand out in the "**Status**" column. It is also used to help with **GDPR consent management** (see "Obtaining consent" section).

Follow the steps below to set up conditional formatting for any word or phrase you would like to stand out.

Select the "**Status**" column. You can do this either by selecting a cell in the column and pressing **Ctrl+Spacebar** or by clicking the letter at the top of the column.

Now select the "**HOME**" menu on the ribbon and click on the "**Conditional Formatting**" tool.

In the drop down menu that appears, select "**Highlight Cells Rules**" and then "**Text that contains…**" (you can also get to this window by pressing **Alt+H,L,H,T**).

In the "**Text That Contains**" window that appears, type the word or phrase you need to be formatted (in the left window under "Format cells that contain the text").

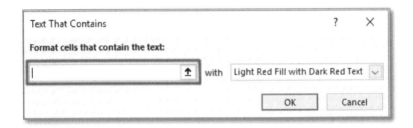

...and then click the arrow to the right of "**Light Red Fill with Dark Red Text**".

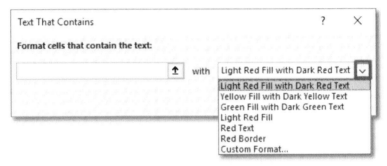

Here you will see some presets to choose from as well as an option at the bottom of the list called "**Custom Format...**" where you can set any formatting you wish.

# Add the final touches

Every note you write in the "**Notes**" column needs to include the date of the interaction. This in the **yyyymmdd** format (ex: **20210503**) so that you can always keep track of exactly when your last interaction happened with a contact. The steps below will help you set up your spreadsheet so that these dates are automatically generated for you. You can also use these dates in the "**Note updates**" and "**Of note**" columns.

First we'll set up a cell so that it contains today's date in the right format.

In your spreadsheet Select **Sheet2** and in **B26** type "**Today:**" then in **B27** type "**=TODAY()**". Press Enter and today's date will appear in cell **B27**. Now in **B23** type "**Source date:**" and in **B24** type "**=TEXT(B27,"yyyymmdd")**" (type the quote marks around "**yyyymmdd**"). The date in **yyyymmdd** format will appear.

Now we have a cell that contains the current date in the format we need (which will update automatically every day). All we have to do now is create notes for our note column that include this date. In **B12** type "**Notes**" and in **B13 through to B21** type the text below:

| Col/Row | Formula to enter into cell |
| --- | --- |
| B13 | =$B$24&": Unavailable " |
| B14 | =$B$24&": No answer " |
| B15 | =$B$24&": Lead - said he/she would be interested to discuss using our services. He/She was happy to meet with/receive a call from and we arranged for this to happen on... " |
| B16 | =$B$24&": VM " |
| B17 | =$B$24&": SB VM " |
| B18 | =$B$24&": Not interested. Would not discuss further. " |

| B19 | =$B$24&": Best person is… Currently unavailable. " |
| B20 | =$B$24&": Will only respond to email. Email sent. " |
| B21 | =$B$24&": Number not working/not correct. " |

Use the data validation method outlined previously to set these date stamped phrases up as menu items in your "**Notes**" and "**Note updates**" column in **Sheet1**. You can also use this method to set up a data validation list option in the "**of note**" column that simply displays today's date in the **yyyymmdd** format.

# The power of filters

At the heart of Excel's power is its ability to let you filter your data very precisely so that you only see what you need to. Once you have set up your columns and headers you can switch on filtering by selecting the whole sheet (**Ctrl+A**) and selecting the "**DATA**" option on the ribbon, and then clicking on the "**Filter**" tool (Shortcuts: **Alt+A,T** or **Ctrl+Shift+L**). You will notice a small arrow appear to the right of each column header.

Clicking on this arrow will open a window that lets you

filter that column based on its contents. You could use this, for example, to filter out any dates from your "**Next action**" column that are in the future so that you don't call certain contacts before you should.

One of the most powerful ways to use filters is to single out certain rows using a simple marker. For example, if you wanted to call only Director level contacts based in London who you haven't spoken to before, you could filter the "**Contact name, role**" column to show only rows with the word "**Director**", filter the "**Address**" column to show only rows with the word "**London**" and then filter the "**Notes**" column to show only blank rows.

If you then chose a different set of filters later on and wanted to come back to this filter set up you would have to filter everything again from the beginning. Alternatively you could set all your filters as needed so that only the data you wanted was displayed and create a new column called "**Director, London, Blank**" and place a "**1**" marker in each cell of that column where that row was displaying data. Now, if you switched all your filters off (**Alt+D,F,S**) or used other filters, you could easily come back to this set up. Just switch on filters again (**Alt+D,F,S**) and filter your new "**Director, London, Blank**" column to show only "**1**".

This avoids having to colour rows of data which can become confusing because then people forget what a certain colour meant. Also sometimes the data is given to other users without explanation. This is how you can end up with data that is full of different coloured columns and rows that no one remembers the meaning of. No one then wants to change that confusing looking formatting as they think it might be important somehow and then you're stuck. My advice would be to, if possible, always choose filtering columns and rows in preference to colouring them.

# GDPR compliance

As mentioned at the start of this book GDPR and ePrivacy are rules governing the methods that you can use to contact your prospects and the specifics of your responsibilities regarding their data. Thankfully there is a straightforward and easy to manage method for doing this efficiently. All the elements you will need are included in the resource pack spreadsheet that you can download by scanning the QR code below:

Or by going to: abbot-davies.com/resource-pack

Password: workshop

**Note**: If you would prefer to build these elements yourself the formulas required are included at the end of this section.

# Obtaining consent

Towards the end of your conversation with a prospect, you will usually offer to send them more information by email. If they say they would be happy for you to do that, you could accept that as consent but it would be hard to prove later unless you are recording the call. The issue you face then, is that you cannot record someone without making them aware of it. This is why so many automated switchboard messages use phrases such as: "Calls may be recorded for training and quality purposes" or "We record all our calls for compliance and security purposes".

To comply with these rules you need to ask them for permission again officially and make them aware that you are recording them (see call recording guide at the end of this section). Once they have indicated that they would be open to receiving your email you should then ask the following question:

**"...and of course because of GDPR I need to record this portion of the call and ask you officially: Can I communicate with you by email?"**

In my experience most people seem to find being asked this question "officially" quite amusing since they have just agreed to it anyway and they usually give their consent without any problem. Once they have given their consent all you need to do is add the date consent was given to the GDPR section of the resource pack spreadsheet:

| GDPR Consent date | GDPR Consent expiry | GDPR Consent expiry (months remaining) | GDPR Opt in evidence |
|---|---|---|---|
| 24/04/2018 | 24/10/2019 | 3 | Recording |
| 08/01/2019 | 08/07/2020 | 12 | Recording |
| 10/06/2019 | 10/12/2020 | 17 | Recording |
| 15/09/2018 | 15/03/2020 | 8 | Recording |
| 05/05/2018 | 05/11/2019 | 4 | Recording |
| 09/02/2019 | 09/08/2020 | 13 | Recording |
| 01/03/2019 | 01/09/2020 | 14 | Recording |
| 25/06/2019 | 25/12/2020 | 18 | Recording |
| 22/07/2018 | 22/01/2020 | 6 | Recording |
| 12/04/2019 | 12/10/2020 | 15 | Recording |
| 03/11/2018 | 03/05/2020 | 10 | Recording |

Let's look at the resource pack spreadsheet now. All the way across to the right of the spreadsheet you will notice four columns with the following titles:

- **GDPR Consent date**
- **GDPR Consent expiry**
- **GDPR Consent expiry (months remaining)**
- **GDPR Opt in evidence**

The cells in the "**GDPR Consent date**" have a menu drop down with today's date as the default selection.

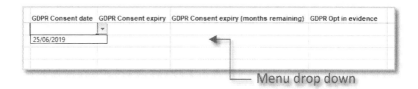

Menu drop down

Simply select this date and press enter. The next two cells to the right will automatically be filled. The first one will show a date eighteen months from the one you have set and the second will show number of months and a progress bar. Eighteen months is the amount of time that an individual's consent to be emailed remains valid.

The "**GDPR Consent expiry (months remaining)**" cell will show the number of months and display a progress bar as a visual cue that will decrease in size from right to left as time goes by.

| GDPR Consent date | GDPR Consent expiry | GDPR Consent expiry (months remaining) |
|---|---|---|
| 25/06/2019 | 25/12/2020 | 18 |

These cells will update every time you load the spreadsheet.

Once you have their consent to be recorded and to receive email you just need to add a hyperlink to the recorded call in the next column titled "**GDPR Opt in evidence**". This way, if there is any query in the future or any audit of your GDPR compliance you can easily provide all the necessary evidence.

Adding a hyperlink to a cell can be done easily by right clicking on the cell you want to hyperlink and choosing the "Link" option. This lets you navigate to your sound file and select it which will then create a clickable link.

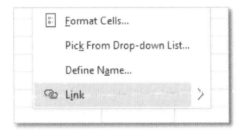

In the future, you can easily check who needs to have their compliance updated simply by filtering the "**GDPR**

**Consent expiry (months remaining)**" column. This will show you contacts whose compliance either has expired or is about to and you can run a campaign just to those contacts to get their consent for another eighteen months.

This system is simple to use and offers a straight forward method for complying with the specific requirements of GDPR as it relates to B2B Telemarketing. More importantly it also helps you support the spirit in which these regulations appear to have been conceived. GDPR is designed to protect businesses from unsolicited emails which I believe is a good thing. It means a few more steps need to be taken for businesses who want to reach out to other businesses but they are worth it if they help reduce the amount of unwanted email (or "spam") every business has to deal with.

**Recording calls**: If you want to use a digital recording as your preferred format for registering consent you will need a phone system that can record calls. If you are already using a VOIP system this is usually quite straight forward and can be done locally on your computer rather than by your VOIP provider. VOIP stands for Voice Over Internet Protocol. It is a system that allows you to make phone calls using your internet connection rather than a phone line. You will need to open an account with a VOIP provider and to download and install some VOIP software. The software is usually not expensive and many VOIP providers will not charge you a monthly fee. Instead these providers offer a "top up" service where you can add money to your account which then only gets used up when you make calls. Their local and national call rates are also usually extremely cheap so a little money will go a very long way. The other big advantage is that VOIP gives you all the functionality of a professional switchboard or company network private branch exchange (PBX) but without the large equipment costs. This is because the functions are cloud based rather than local so you don't have to buy, maintain or upgrade any costly equipment.

**Formulas in this section:**

[**GDPR Consent expiry**] - Used to calculate a date eighteen months from date GDPR consent was given:

=DATE(YEAR(O2), MONTH(O2) + 18, DAY(O2))

The O2 reference in this formula is only used as an example here. It refers to the cell that contains the date consent was given. In the resource pack spreadsheet this cell is directly to the left of the one containing this formula. Edit as required.

[**GDPR Consent expiry (months remaining)**] - Used to display the number of months remaining:

=IF(TODAY()<>"",DATEDIF(TODAY(), P2,"m"),"")

As before, the P2 reference in this formula is only used as an example. It refers to the cell that contains the consent expiry date. In the resource pack spreadsheet this cell is directly to the left of the one containing this formula. Edit as required.

The progress bar is added simply by selecting the whole column where you would like progress bars to display and selecting the following options on the ribbon:

**Home → Conditional Formatting → Data Bars → Gradient fill**

*(Shortcut: Alt H, L, D)*

...then finally selecting the type and colour of gradient bar preferred.

# The
# "How do I stay focused?"
## Monster

Stress ruins everything. Fear and anxiety that is either felt immediately or builds up over time can freeze you up and trigger all sorts of negative reactions. Procrastination, feeling stupid, disliked, or just not up to the task are a few that may be familiar. After a few dozen calls that have not gone well, as is sometimes inevitable, you may start to experience some or all of these. They are certainly things I have battled with for as long as I have been in the B2B Telemarketing business. You can't just make these problems go away but you can "re-label" them.

As someone once explained to me when I first started making B2B calls, imagine you need to dig a hole but it's a hot day and you're tired and you just don't want to, you could give up OR you could turn "**I don't want to dig a hole**" into:

- I'm **NOT** digging a hole, I'm just... playing with this shovel.

- I'm **NOT** digging a hole, I'm only... sticking the shovel in the ground because it's fun to stand on it and watch it sink in.

- I'm **NOT** digging a hole, I'm just... pulling the shovel back and lifting some earth up because there's sometimes interesting stuff that comes up.

**Oh look, a hole!**

The key is to break the thing that you don't want to do into steps. It's far more likely that you will follow a few small steps than one huge one and most importantly it **keeps you moving**. When we are stressed we stop moving and even stop breathing properly. As the journalist and author **Robert Heller** once said:

**"Fear is excitement without breath"**

# Breathe the stress out

There is a simple breathing technique I found some years ago that can really help reduce the tension and can also be done discreetly at any time of the day. It is used by many different types of professional people including high level management staff, government employees (and the armed forces who refer to it as "Tactical Breathing" but then they would, wouldn't they). You can do this in a standing or sitting position and, if you are not able to find a quiet space, that's fine.

Start by breathing out slowly...

Breathe in for three seconds...
Hold your breath for three seconds...
Breathe out for three seconds...
Relax, repeat.

The length of time is up to you so long as each segment **in/hold/out** is the **same length** and you feel comfortable doing it. It only usually takes a few of these breaths to noticeably improve your sense of calm and focus.

If your environment permits, you can also add a point of focus for your mind while you do these exercises by putting your hands together as though praying and then pulling your palms apart so that just the tips of your fingers and your thumbs are touching. This will form a triangle. Focus on one of the corners (I tend to start with the bottom left corner) and as you breathe in move you gaze clockwise to the next corner. Now as you hold your breath, move your gaze to the next corner again. Finally, as you breathe out move you gaze back to where you started.

# Wake up your speaking muscles

Before you even pick up the phone the pitch, volume, rhythm, and timbre of your voice is going to set the stage. The more confident and relaxed you sound, the better. If the muscles of your mouth are stiff, tight or cramped that is exactly how your voice is going to sound.

Actors and singers often prepare their voices using **vocal warm up exercises**. These help them with the physical demands of speaking or singing clearly and audibly in front of an audience for long periods of time. These simple exercises are fun to do and will help you sound more confident on the phone. They are also a great way of generally raising your energy. Try repeating each of the phrases below **three times**. Really enunciate each word to stretch those muscles.

**Two toads, terribly tired,
trying to trot to Tewksbury**

**Unique New York
New York Unique**

**She stood on the balcony,
inexplicably mimicking him hiccupping,
and amicably welcoming him home.**

This old nursery rhyme is also a great warm up exercise.

## I like the flowers

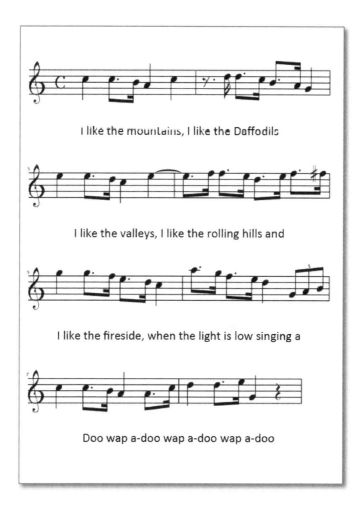

I like the mountains, I like the Daffodils

I like the valleys, I like the rolling hills and

I like the fireside, when the light is low singing a

Doo wap a-doo wap a-doo wap a-doo

# Practice difficult names and words

If you notice that you are about to call a number where you will have to say a potentially difficult-to-pronounce word or name, it makes sense to practice it beforehand.

Starting a call with:

**"May I speak to Mr Subra… Subramannam… erm… Soobramaniam… sorry… Subramanian?"**

Isn't a great way to begin a conversation.

If you stumble over your words you will increase your chances of being identified as a cold caller. You want to try to sound as though these names are familiar to you. This will not only make you sound less like a cold caller but it will also help increase the gatekeeper's confidence in you as a caller they might want to keep talking to.

# Consider standing up

Standing up while making calls is a great way to keep your energy up and stay positive. When you stand you are more nimble. If someone tries to push you off balance you can more easily recover. The same thing is true psychologically. It's a lot easier to deal with unexpected questions or negative reactions if you're on your feet. If you have a run of calls where everyone is being negative you can bounce back a lot easier if you're standing.

You will probably also find that your productivity and focus increase as it's much harder to waste time on unproductive activities when you're standing. If you're sitting it's easy to start slouching and switch your brain off. Ideally you might also reconfigure your desk so that your keyboard, mouse and monitor are at waist height. This way you can type and use your mouse without having to bend down and interrupt your flow.

There are also several health concerns connected with sitting down too much that include an increased risk of heart disease, cancer and type two diabetes. In short, standing is a great way to give yourself the best chance of staying focused, positive and healthy while you make those calls.

It used to be the case that standing desks came at a premium as they were often regarded as specialist items for people with back problems that required custom made ergonomic solutions. As more businesses have begun to realise the health benefits of standing up this is no longer the case. I would personally recommend looking at IKEA's **BEKANT** range of height adjustable desks (**https://www.ikea.com/gb/en/cat/office-desks-18962/**). I have used this type of desk for many years and they have always been very reliable and easy to use. They also feature a motorised raising and lowering mechanism that saves time and effort and compared to what desks like this used to cost they really are very good value.

# Some final thoughts

With this book I have tried to create a simple but useful guide through the potentially "Monster" filled world of the B2B telemarketing landscape. Hopefully, here you have found many useful strategies that will help you produce a steady stream of valuable leads.

We looked at the importance of taking the time to really understand your market and your prospects and how easy it is to get started. We examined the challenges of the gatekeeper and the needs of the key decision maker, what to say to both and how to structure that information to really get your message across. We explored methods for keeping track of the work you are doing so that nothing is wasted and you are always able to get to the information you need. Finally we looked at different ways to avoid letting stress get in the way of your calling.

There is no doubt that producing high quality leads in a sustainable way takes practice. The best advice I can give is that, no matter what, keep going. I'm not suggesting that you keep smacking your head against a brick wall though. If you make fifty calls and you can see that you're not getting anywhere, look at your approach and see if there are adjustments you could make. Maybe call a different market sector or focus on a different job role. Not getting anywhere with Marketing Directors in the Financial sector? Try Office Managers or switch to the Insurance sector for the next fifty calls. Just made seventy calls that didn't go well? Filter your spreadsheet to show only your friendly, more receptive

"**Nurture**" contacts and use the "**Next action**" column to see if there are any who are available to call today. Did you notice that a word or phrase in your **Direct Value Statement** is making people audibly sigh? Look at your **LOVE** and **FEAR** buckets and change it.

The ability to keep going but also to adapt and change your approach as you start to understand more clearly what works and what doesn't is a very powerful combination. A lot of people pick one strategy and just hammer it out until they are so jaded and tired that you can hear it in their voices when they call you. That in itself becomes part of the problem as well and often this leads to an unsuccessful outcome.

Stay nimble, keep on trucking and you too will soon **Conquer the Telephone Monster®**.

For more information about signing up to the workshops, one on one tuition, answers to any questions you may have or to send feedback to the author about this book please visit

# www.abbot-davies.com

You can also find us on Facebook at Abbot-Davies Associates and Twitter at @ADLeadgen.

# Toolbox

This is a brief technical guide based on the equipment and software I use myself.

Unless you are tied into a landline based system for geographical or contractual reasons I would strongly recommend that you consider using a VOIP solution for your calling. VOIP is so much more flexible and affordable than professional switchboard or company network **private branch exchange** (PBX) systems. It's true to say that in the past there were issues with call quality because of the uneven speeds with which businesses accessed the internet. However, today even the cheapest, most basic internet connection usually has more than enough bandwidth to ensure that call quality should be undistinguishable from landline calls. Also VOIP accounts allow you to choose a phone number that will display on caller ID systems and that people can call from any phone.

**Note**: You should not intentionally misrepresent your location by choosing a number that appears to be from an area other than where you are based. In any case, I believe most VOIP providers will now insist that you choose a number that is within the area code of your registered business.

Using VOIP does not mean you can't have a physical phone on your desk to use if that's what you are comfortable with. There are many different kinds of so called "IP" desk phones and the type I have used very successfully for many years are the **D3XX Series IP phones from Snom Technology (https://www.snom.com/ip-phones/desk-phones/d3xx-series/)**.

If, instead you would rather use a software based phone or "Soft" phone I have had excellent results with an application called **Zoiper** (**https://www.zoiper.com/**). Again there are many choices but Zoiper has always worked very well for me, allows native call recording (see "Obtaining consent" section for compliance info) and has a trial version that is free.

Compared to landlines, the other hurdle that soft phones let you jump quite easily has to do with headsets. There are two types of headsets for telemarketing: **Monaural** and **Binaural.** Both are worn on your head but **monaural** only has one functioning earpiece like a traditional desk phone. I am a strong advocate of using **binaural** headsets because this way you hear the person you are talking to in the centre of your head. This feels more natural and because you spend most of your life hearing people's voices this way rather than in just one ear it will help you relax more and talk more naturally.

It is easy to find binaural headsets for "Soft" phones because regular computer headsets are naturally binaural. All you are doing with a "Soft" phone is using your computers normal headset and microphone. Also because computer headsets are a very common item, available almost everywhere, they are usually quite affordable. I would recommend the **Logitech H390 USB Computer Headset** (**https://www.logitech.com/en-gb/product/usb-headset-h390**). It is very durable, comfortable and comes with noise cancelling technology which helps if you are making calls in an environment that isn't quiet.

# Terminology

Below is a guide to the terminology used in this book:

**Contact**
A general term to describe someone within an organisation or a business.

**Gatekeeper**
A person within an organisation or business who can decide whether to pass a call through to a potential decision maker (or not!).

**Prospect**
A Contact who…
…fits your ideal type of client.

**Nurture**
A prospect who…
…is the right person within a business to talk to about your offering.
…has expressed an interest in your product or service.
…is not ready at this stage to meet or receive a call to discuss using your services but is happy to receive more information and/or a follow up call at a later date.

**Lead**
A prospect who…
…is the right person within a business to talk to about your

offering.

...has expressed an interest in your product.

...has agreed to a face to face meeting or to receiving a call to discuss using your services.

## Qualified out

This describes a contact who...

...is not interested in using your services and is unwilling to discuss things further.

...and/or is not interested in receiving any further communication from you.

...and/or is unable to use your services for the foreseeable future due to circumstances beyond their control (long term contract, going out of business).

## Email only

This describes a prospect who will only accept contact by email.

## VM/SBVM

These are the only two abbreviations used in the spreadsheet section of this book. Abbreviations should be kept to a minimum in any note taking so that your work can easily be shared with others.

VM is Voicemail - e.g. "Hi this is John Smith. I'm sorry I can't take your call. Please leave a message."

SBVM is Switchboard Voicemail - e.g. "I'm sorry no one is available to take your call. Please leave a message and someone will call you back as soon as possible."

**VOIP**

This stands for Voice Over Internet Protocol – It is a system that allows you to make and receive phone calls using your internet connection instead of a standard phone line.

# About the Author

**Orion Abbot-Davies** was plunged into the choppy waters of B2B telemarketing during the economic meltdown of 2008. His experiences during those chaotic years left him with a strong desire to help others see why they don't need to be nervous about cold calling. Writing a **step by step guide** that would show his readers how, by the end of a single day, they could have a telemarketing campaign ready to go was always a dream. "**Conquer the Telephone Monster®**" has made that dream a reality and offers its readers all the tools they need to know who to call, what to say, how to charm gatekeepers, how to deal with objections, how to close and a host of other **expert tips**.

Printed in Poland
by Amazon Fulfillment
Poland Sp. z o.o., Wrocław